Angels & Entrepreneurs
The standard reference for people considering Angel Investing

ANGELS&
ENTREPRENEURS

The standard reference for people
considering **Angel Investing**

Jonathan Harrison FCA FInstD

Angels and Entrepreneurs
The standard reference for people considering Angel Investing

First published in 2011 by
Ecademy Press
48 St Vincent Drive, St Albans, Herts, AL1 5SJ
info@ecademy-press.com
www.ecademy-press.com

Printed and bound by Lightning Source in the UK and USA
Designed by Michael Inns
Artwork by Karen Gladwell

Printed on acid-free paper from managed forests. This book is printed on demand, so no copies will be remaindered or pulped.

ISBN 978-1-907722-59-2

The right of Jonathan Harrison to be identified as the author of this work has been inserted in accordance with sections 77 and 78 of the Copyright Designs and Patents Act 1988.

A CIP catalogue record for this book is available from the British Library.

This book is available online and all good bookstores.

Contents

Acknowledgements

I wish to thank Mindy Gibbins-Klein of *the book midwife* fame for providing some of her time in 2008, having completed a first draft of my book *Life's Hop, Skip and a Jump* which was published in December 2008 (available from **www.lulu.com** or **www.amazon. com**) that describes my life experiences and learning while travelling the world and migrating from the corporate ladder to an entrepreneurial career.

We met again in June 2011 at an Ecademy meeting (**www. ecademy.com**) when we exchanged my book for her book "24 Carat BOLD" which after reading that weekend, encouraged me to continue to complete writing this book following my own experience of angel investing.

I also wish to thanks the two New Zealanders, Richard Stubbs and Martin Hickman, for their honesty, hard work, perseverance, giving me the opportunity to invest, and the fun we had over five years while developing UK Explorer Limited that I have used as one of my case studies in chapter 10. In addition, thanks to Michael Kennedy for having faith in the UK Explorer team when approached to provide a venture capital financing.

In addition, I wish to thank Winton G. Rossiter, the founder of JazzyMedia and Weight Wins, for his contribution to my chapter "What should an Entrepreneur look for in a Business Angel", and for the opportunity to make my fifth Angel investment in his early stage company Weight Wins.

Lastly, but not least, to my wife Mariela for having faith and supporting me during many difficult years after the sale of my successful management buy in ("MBI") of twenty five UK hotels, after which I went out on my own to search and become involved in different entrepreneurial opportunities.

Introduction

I hope this book will help anyone considering making an Angel Investment for the first time, to avoid the many pitfalls through the usual trial and error that most Business Angels experience. In addition, I hope this will also help an Entrepreneur to understand what a Business Angel looks at when considering such an investment. This has been taken from my own practical business experience and specifically my own experience of Angel investing. This book refers mainly to UK organizations, although there are some statistics in chapter 9 relating to the USA and Canada.

If a person has surplus financial capital, which they can afford to risk for a "high risk – high reward" opportunity, then they may be tempted to become a Business Angel, which is not for the faint hearted! It is often quoted that only one in ten Angel investments is likely to be successful.

With UK interest rates likely to remain low for some time, it is very tempting to try and leverage surplus capital by investing in a business with the hope of a significant future capital gain – it's a lot more difficult to actually achieve this!

After a successful £92m management buy in ("MBI") and exit 22 months later, I have personally invested as a Business Angel in one start-up and four early stage companies. This book has been developed drawing from this experience. I am continuously looking for the next opportunity, and as a rule of thumb, I probably seriously look at one or two in every hundred or so executive summaries that I review in a year.

What is an Entrepreneur?

The English dictionary describes an Entrepreneur as "the owner or manager of a business enterprise who, by risk, initiative, attempts to make profits".

Charles and Elizabeth Handy's description of Entrepreneurs is the "New Alchemists, creating something of value out of nothing"!

I would add that it is somebody with a creative mind, the ability to generate ideas, research them, and see a material market opportunity as a first mover in that market. An Entrepreneur also has to have patience, perseverance, tenacity and endurance to see through the development of the opportunity, and have a multitude of skills being analytical, personable, their own sales person, and in areas they have a lack of experience, know how to find experienced people to believe in their opportunity and support them to succeed.

An Entrepreneur has to have patience, perseverance, tenacity and endurance

What is a Business Angel?

A Business Angel is an investor in a business venture that requires additional funding and tends to be at the start-up or in the early stages of the life of a business with potential for high growth, although it could equally apply to saving a well-established business that is unable to obtain bank loans.

This book is only devoted to start-up and early stage businesses, although most of these matters equally apply to a well-established business, but may well require a much greater amount of due diligence.

Business Angel investment is normally in the form of equity finance, rather than loans, and typically Business Angels invest their own funds, unlike venture capitalists that manage the pooled money of others in a professionally managed fund.

A typical active Business Angel will tend to make one or two investments during a year, and where they are the sole investor or the "Lead Investor" (sometimes referred to as an "archangel") they will often wish to take an active part in the business using their prior business experience and contacts whether in the same industry or business sector or not. They will get a certain amount of enjoyment from the future success of the business and a sense of well being putting something back.

A Business Angel must have patience, be supportive and able to lose their investment

What does this book have to offer?

This book gives an overview of a typical business funding cycle, where to find suitable opportunities, facts that a Business Angel should initially review for pre-selection, what an Entrepreneur should look for in a Business Angel, what due diligence the Business Angel should carry out before investing, what should be in the Shareholder Agreement, how does the Business Angel achieve an exit, the chances of a successful exit, Business Angel investing statistics, two case studies of Angel investments made by myself based on an actual successful exit and an unsuccessful exit, three check lists and two flow charts.

CHAPTER ONE

Where does Angel investment fit into the business funding cycle?

All successful businesses will go through the below mentioned funding cycles, provided of course the Entrepreneurs continuously adapt and develop their service and/or products to survive in an ever, fast changing, environment. While this is not an exhaustive list of possible funding, it provides the main fund raising steps, some of which may be skipped depending on the progress in developing the business.

Entrepreneurs direct Funding

Usually, Entrepreneurs start their businesses on the basis of "Bootstrapping" (an American term) where they do everything to minimize the costs of starting their business such as work from home or borrow rent free office space, borrow equipment, ask for free support and advice from their business friends and from within their networks, etc. They also use their own limited financial resources where they have some, and in some cases use credit cards to pay for costs, which they cannot pay for out of their own direct resources, resulting in building up debt to the maximum of their credit card limit. Although this shows commitment, this is a very risky and expensive approach that should be avoided!

I know of one person who spent five years developing a safety product that he had patented and for which he received a great deal of publicity, but this resulted in him increasing the mortgage on his house to the absolute maximum, run up debts on his credit cards and take loans received from friends. When I met him, having reached a prototype stage and having expressions of interest from retailers, he was struggling to obtain the funding for the tooling and working capital to bring this product to the market. This situation is not unusual and requires a great deal of self-belief, perseverance and tenacity.

Friends and Family Funding

The next stage of funding is usually by begging support from friends and family, if available, often referred to as "friends, family and fools" ("FFF")! However, this is usually only a stopgap before obtaining Business Angel funding, as most frequently amounts raised at this stage will be small, although often adequate enough to develop an idea or product to present to Business Angels.

Investment Grants

It is sometimes possible to obtain investment grants in certain regions of the country for certain types of development, but often this requires generating a great deal of documentation, form filling and the inevitable lobbying. This will usually result in a lot of valuable time being spent by the Entrepreneur, who really needs to be focused on the development of the business idea, and where speed to market may need to be given priority.

The Entrepreneur must weigh up value of a grant against speed to market

There are people who specialize in helping Entrepreneurs to file claims for grants on a "no win-no fee" basis, but of course that reduces the net amount of the grant. There is a grant website at **www.grantaid.com** that covers the full spectrum of business grants should the Entrepreneurs and Business Angels wish to explore this area further.

Seed Capital

Seed Capital is described in the English dictionary as "money used for the establishment of an enterprise". This normally refers to the first fund raising after an Entrepreneur has developed an idea or product that they wish to bring to the market, having used up their own resources to reach this stage. This type of funding may also replace the need to access friends and family for financial support.

This usually entails one Angel investor providing this first round of funds which should allow the business to get properly started with proper business premises, ability to file patents and Intellectual Property (IP) protection, provide for some proper administration and possibly to allow the Entrepreneur to be paid a very modest salary.

The Business Angel should expect, at a later date, to have to provide several tranches of additional capital as the business develops, particularly if the Business Angel wishes to avoid dilution of their investment.

Business Angel Funding

Business Angel capital fills the gap in the initial start-up financing between "Friends and Family" and/or "Seed Capital" funding and "Venture Capital" funding, which are referred to above and below respectively.

Business Angel investment can be provided by a single investor, or a group of investors, known as a "Syndicate". Business Angels tend to be people who have individual wealth, a lottery win, inheritance and/or had prior financial success through investment or managing businesses themselves.

If a Syndicate of Angel Investors is chosen, then the Entrepreneur should insist that only one person from the Syndicate be appointed as the "Lead Investor", with responsibility for liaison with the Entrepreneur on behalf of the other Syndicate investors and should be a person that the Entrepreneur has a good rapport with.

Business Angels typically will invest between £10,000 and £1 million in a business opportunity, with the larger amounts by a sole Business Angel, and will depend upon whether the business is at a start-up stage or actually generating early stage revenue. Syndicate Investors will typically contribute between £10,000 and £50,000 to a Syndicate, although £10,000 to £20,000 appears to be the norm.

Syndicate funding lowers the amount of exposure to risk by the Syndicate investors, however it also reduces the ability to influence the direction of the business and the amount of future reward on the success of the business.

The Entrepreneur should consider whether to have one investor or a Syndicate of investors, obviously depending on the ease of the availability of funds at any one time from the Business Angel networks. Naturally, the top agenda is to raise the cash!

Also the Entrepreneur should consider whether the sole Business Angel or Lead Investor, has previous business experience and can add some value in the areas of industry contacts, a professional background such as PR, marketing, accounting, legal, engineering or these types of disciplines as appropriate for the business, which can all lead to reduced costs in the early stages of the business's development.

In addition to cash, can the Business Angel or Lead Investor add value?

With a Syndicate, the Entrepreneur should appoint a Lead Investor, who can also provide the same type of support and channel all updates on the businesses progress to the other investors between each of the annual results reports. Unfortunately, in many cases, despite the appointment of a Lead Investor, the Entrepreneur will find that they have to field telephone calls and meetings from the other investors, particularly as it is unusual for all the Syndicate investors' individual investment criteria to be aligned.

As a Business Angel, I personally prefer to be the only investor provided that I can fulfill the funding requirements, as it avoids the above mentioned Syndicate issues and enables myself to have an on going, one to one relationship, with the Entrepreneur enabling them to be entirely focused on the development of the business. This also enables me to have fun providing mentoring, any other specialist support that I may be able to add, and working my contacts.

The Entrepreneur needs to consider all of the above alongside the availability of funding and the relationship being developed with the individual Business Angels during the initial contacts and discussion.

Subsequent Business Angel Funding Rounds

As a Business Angel, it is quite normal to experience subsequent funding round requests, following on from an initial Angel investment of up to three times. It is therefore important that Business Angels who invest consider this if they wish to avoid dilution or in a worst-case scenario, a failure of the business without these additional funds. Naturally, the Business Angel will not desire to do so if the relationship with the Entrepreneur is strained or there is a disagreement on the future direction of the business.

Business Angels should be able to fund future funding rounds to avoid dilution

Likewise, the Entrepreneur should check the future funding ability of the Business Angel. In addition, if you are unable to provide additional funding and ignoring future dilution, this will lead to the Entrepreneur having to devote a lot of time to an additional fund raise and they may lose their primary focus on the businesses development.

If the Angel Investor(s) is not willing to invest further, this may put off potential new investors. In a worst-case scenario, if the Entrepreneur and Angel Investor cannot attract additional capital, this could lead to the failure of the business.

Venture Capital Trusts ("Super Angels")

The AngelNews, referred to below in chapter 2, has highlighted a new category of Business Angels, Venture Capital Trusts ("VCT") and Family Offices, known as "Super Angels". These VCT's are pools of funds, belonging to individual investors who wish to spread their risk, and are set up to benefit from UK tax concessions for selected types of business. The UK Chancellor of the Exchequer has indicated that he will broaden the scope of businesses covered by these tax concessions from April 2012.

It is important to know which VCT's to be approached as some specialize in specific areas, while others are generalists. They can be approached for funding of much larger amounts than Business Angels can generally provide. VCT's include New Wave Ventures (**www.nwventures.co.uk**), Horatio Investments (**www.horatioinvestments.com**), Hotspur Capital Partners (no website), Braveheart Ventures in the UK's North East, Avonmore Developments in the UK's South East tech scene, Beringea's ProVen Growth & Income, ISIS's Baronsmead, Climate Change Capital, Foresight, Hotbed, Downing, Octopus Capital and Pi Capital, all of whom are actively investing in early stage companies.

These VCT's are not interested in companies entering existing markets where they are effectively copying a successful business, particularly if they would be competing against a much larger business. All VCT's look for good a good management team and will help to add to the team in specialist areas, such as the finance department.

VCT's look for a strong management team and robust internal controls

Other Temporary Sources of Funding

Other forms of funding such as Lease Finance for and secured on physical equipment, and Invoice Financing can generally be used once a business has some substance, but this source of funding is expensive although it does avoid further shareholder equity dilution.

Small Firms Loan Guarantee Scheme ("SFLG")

The SFLG is a joint venture between the UK Department of Tourism and Industry ("DTI") and a number of UK high street banks that will lend up to £250,000 over a period of 10 years where a company has an annual turnover below £5.6m and is not more than five years old.

An application form is available from banks and you can expect to pay relatively high interest rates. My previous experience of this was that the banks are still very reluctant to lend, as they only receive a government guarantee on part of the loan being made.

Fast track Funding

There are some cases where speed to market is essential, when it would be better for the Entrepreneur to seek out potential Angel Investors, who have both the resources and experience of raising material sums of money from venture capital companies or on a pre IPO basis, with the ability to quickly list the company on the Alternative Investment Market "AIM" of the London Stock Exchange referred to below. Listing on AIM is only really worthwhile if the Entrepreneur needs a significant cash injection to materially gear up the business.

> *Where speed to market is essential, consider fast track funding despite the dilution*

This cuts out the need to consider the steps of the Business Growth Fund, venture capital and bank loans noted below, and will most likely result in the Entrepreneur creating greater value, faster, although resulting in dilution of the Entrepreneurs equity.

Business Growth Fund ("BGF")

The UK government has persuaded the main British banks to launch the Business Growth Fund in April 2012 that will eventually have £2.5 billion pounds to invest and with offices in Birmingham, Bristol, Edinburgh, London and Manchester. It appears that they have a skeleton staff at present and are still developing the details of what business types they will invest in and the conditions that they will impose.

The stated criteria are that the investee companies must be capable of rapid growth, with BGF looking to invest between £2 million to £10 million per company, and it is believed that it may not necessarily be looking for an exit in three to seven years, as many private equity investors demand. This will eliminate the opportunity for many businesses backed by Business Angels to use BGF, as they will need to have grown very fast in the first few years to be able to benefit from this minimum level of funding.

Stephen Welton, the BGF CEO, expects that it will invest in one of ten applicant companies and will offer advice and signposting to other relevant sources of finance or advice to the unsuccessful companies.

It does seem that BGF will not fulfill the needs of early stage businesses at all and appears to place BGF to being closer to the profile of the smaller venture capital firms.

Venture Capital Funding

In the English dictionary, "Venture Capital", also known as "Risk Capital", is described as "capital that is provided for a new commercial enterprise by individuals or organizations other than those who own the new enterprise".

You would not normally approach a Venture Capital firm before your business has a revenue stream or a revenue generating contract, is ideally making profits and with the potential to significantly increase the profitability by ramping up activity through further investment. It is possible to negotiate the sale of a portion of your equity for cash as well as obtain a repayable, interest bearing, loan from a Venture Capital firm, where the loan portion can be used as a safety net in case the cost of development or investment in new equipment exceeds the Entrepreneurs initial estimation for a major expansion or project. This approach also reduces the amount of dilution the Entrepreneur must endure.

There are numerous Venture Capital firms that can be found through the British Venture Capital Association at **www.bvca.co.uk** or similar organizations in the country in which you are operational.

In order to narrow down an appropriate Venture Capital firm, the Entrepreneur needs to establish what industry types the venture capital firms are interested in and the level of funding that they indicate they are willing to invest, which can usually be found on their websites. However, the Entrepreneur will find that many have a wide description of businesses they are willing to invest in so as to not discourage enquiries, but many tend to really only specialize in one or two sectors.

An alternative, is to talk to somebody you know who has had dealings with Venture Capital firms, such as myself, who may know somebody appropriate for your company's size and sector.

Talk to somebody you know who has experience of venture capital funding

Venture Capital firms look for an experienced management team, as well as the business type and opportunity, and may insist that the team is strengthened with specific skills that they may feel are missing. They will also expect that there is a professional approach to monthly accounting and robust internal controls, which they will review in detail during their due diligence.

Bank Loans

At the time of the publication of this book, bank loans are extremely difficult to obtain, if not impossible, in the current financial climate for a young company, and will certainly not be achievable unless the company is profitable and has some material collateral, such as property, and a well known business investor and backer such as a Venture Capital firm. This generally rules out bank loans until material revenue streams and profitability are proven.

Initial Public Offering (IPO)

There are three ways to complete an IPO in the UK that may be dictated by the size, industry sector, revenue and profitability now and projected for the future. They all require a host of costly advisors to review and advise on the Offer Document, known as a "Prospectus", to protect the board of directors and after the IPO advise on the ongoing communication with investors. These are a Nominated Advisor ("Nomad") for AIM or a "Sponsor" for the main market, lawyer, accountant, broker, financial PR firm, prospectus printer and registrar.

The Entrepreneur needs to be really committed to go for an IPO

In order to achieve a successful IPO, the company needs to have professional, supportive advisors, an experienced management team, good administration and audited accounts for the last three years of the company's history, or shorter if the company was formed during this timeframe, otherwise the costs of producing the Offer Document will be excessive. In addition, where new funds are raised, you will normally have to pay 5% to 6% of the amount raised in commission on top of all the advisor fees. As a safety net, past experience has led me to expect the overall costs to be in excess of those initially quoted by the various advisors, and the company should ensure it has sufficient funds before proceeding with an IPO.

Expect IPO advisor costs to be higher than the Entrepreneur is used to

The Entrepreneur will have to spend a considerable amount of time networking and talking to the above type of professional advisors. A Business Angel with experience in this area, such as myself, would be able to support the Entrepreneur in this activity. It is normal to request potential advisors, with whom the Entrepreneur has developed a rapport, to present to the board of directors in what is know as a "beauty parade", at which they should disclose their fee proposals, before deciding on the final list of advisors to list the company.

The advisors will do their own due diligence before agreeing to act for the company, and request all the board directors, and possibly key management, to complete a due diligence form and satisfy the Money Laundering Regulations.

It is also possible, depending upon the circumstances, for the directors and management to negotiate with the Nomad or Sponsor to use this opportunity to sell some of their equity at the price struck for the listing. However, this can leave a negative message for potential investors and should be avoided if at all possible.

Plus Markets ("Plus")

Plus is a junior market in which share transactions are matched and is used by very small companies to raise relatively small amounts of capital, somewhere between £500,000 and £5m. The cost of listing on the Plus is the least expensive of the three UK markets and requires less preparation, but higher as a percentage of the capital raised, and the annual fees are higher than those for AIM at the time of going to print. In addition, liquidity on Plus is very poor and over the last few years, numerous small companies have subsequently delisted during the UK's recent economic down turn as they have often been unable to raise additional funds due to this lack of liquidity.

Plus's liquidity is very poor and many companies have delisted

From my own practical experience, I would recommend the Alternative Investment Market ("AIM") is considered in preference to Plus, whenever possible.

Alternative Investment Market (AIM)

AIM is the junior market of the London Stock Exchange and is a more liquid market than Plus, provided the company has the ability to announce frequent and positive news-flows, can produce above average ongoing growth for their industry sector and can fund the commissions of analysts reports.

The cost of listing on AIM is much higher than Plus, but is generally lower as a percentage of the capital raised. The ongoing annual costs of maintaining an AIM listing are higher than Plus and are at least between approximately £100,000 and £150,000 for smaller companies. These costs cover the ongoing advisor fees mentioned above, interim and annual reports, listing share prices in the press, regulatory announcements, analysts reports, financial PR, etc.

AIM companies need to produce above average ongoing growth and shout about this

It is important to note that AIM has much more flexible regulations than the main market, discussed below, although this has been tightened up over the last few years. The advantage of listing on AIM, besides easing the ability to raise additional funds, increasing the companies profile and improving the company's perceived credibility, is that the company is able to use marketable shares to acquire other businesses rather than just cash. However, many of the UK financial institutions will be unable to invest in AIM companies as their investment criteria does not allow them to.

One advantage of an AIM listing for both the Entrepreneur and Business Angel is that under current tax legislation, AIM company shareholdings are exempt from inheritance tax in the UK. This may be particularly relevant to elderly Entrepreneurs and Business Angels who wish to leave the business and/or their wealth to their family without their inheritors having to sell the business to settle an inheritance tax liability. If the Business Angel is resident in another country, it is worth exploring whether there may also be similar beneficial terms for investments in early stage companies.

London Stock Exchange (Main market)

Normally, only much larger companies go straight to the main market, as they will have the financial resources to pay the higher costs of advisors and the Prospectus. However, if an early stage company can manage to raise a sufficiently large amount of pre IPO money, it may well be able to join the main market without stepping through AIM, provided the company is of a creditable size, has an experienced management team and the ability to quickly further develop its' business.

If the company can raise sufficient pre IPO money, it may be able to join the main market

As AIM listed companies develop and their share price improves with performance, a logical step is to migrate to the main market which further increases the company's market creditability, opens up the ability for Financial Institutions to invest, increases the liquidity and the ability to raise additional funds.

The regulatory requirements of the main market are much more onerous and more costly on an ongoing basis. However, this makes a company much stronger, adds the ability to issue very marketable shares for acquisitions, and generally makes it much easier to borrow from the banks at lower interest rates when required.

Overseas stock exchanges

I make no comment on other stock exchanges as I have had limited practical experience, but they should not be ignored, particularly if the company has a strong trading position in a particular country or wishes to increase its exposure in another country. Many companies wishing to enter or strengthen their position in, for example, China, will obtain a primary or secondary listing in Hong Kong. It is possible to have a number of stock exchange listings but this is normally reserved for much larger companies.

CHAPTER TWO

Where do you find early stage businesses requiring funding?

There are plenty of small businesses looking for funding at any one time, and active Angel Investors will look at as many as one hundred or more opportunities every year, with only one or two being pursued. This is often because many Entrepreneurs present their proposition very poorly, are ill prepared and do not present themselves professionally. If you have seen any of the series of the television program "Dragons Den", you will have seen clear evidence of this. However, in my view, Business Angels should not use this as an example of how to deal with Entrepreneurs!

The worst thing Entrepreneurs can do, is to make contact with potential investors before being properly prepared, as they have only once chance and a few minutes to make an impression, and generally they will not get a second chance.

An Angel Investor who manages to invest before the Entrepreneur approaches any of the organizations noted below, may well be able to obtain a lower valuation for their investment

The one personal dislike I have, is that once these early stage businesses approach the organizations mentioned below, there is a cost of this support, being a fee of at least £5,000 for help to prepare or tidy up the Entrepreneurs presentation and executive summary, and to provide a venue at which they can professionally present their opportunity, plus a further 5% or more of the funds raised.

I express this view because if the Entrepreneur fails to find suitable investors within a particular Angel network, they will have paid the initial fee when they have limited or non-existent resources. I would like to see a higher "success only fee" based on the actual funds raised as being more equitable, which should encourage the relevant networks to work harder on behalf of the Entrepreneur.

It is very difficult to assess the value of start-ups and early stage businesses and these organizations also tend to result in pushing up the Entrepreneurs valuation expectations. The Entrepreneur needs to be flexible for the right fit of Angel Investor(s) that may be overlooked due to the dire need for funding!

Networking

Networking is one way for potential Business Angels to find opportunities, as well as research into what is actually happening in the small business arena. There are numerous ways to do this, such as join organizations like **www.ecademy.com**, **www.linkedin.com** or the many others, some of which hold Angel investor meetings and presentations by professional advisors.

Potential Business Angels should also make contact with banks, lawyers, accountants, PR firms and other advisors who often know of small businesses looking for funding. Some of these parties may also be members of Angel networks and provide meeting space in their offices for the Angel networks' Entrepreneurs to present their propositions and offer advice.

British Business Angels Association (BBAA)

The British Business Angels Association (**www.bbaa.org.uk**), or similar organizations in other countries, can provide potential Business Angels with details of all the registered Angel networks in your country. If a potential Business Angel is considering Angel investing, and to enable them to experience the process and network with other Business Angels, I recommend that they join their local Angel network to attend their meetings at which a number of Entrepreneurs will usually present their propositions for investment.

These networks usually help guide the Entrepreneur to develop a professional presentation, executive summary and enable potential Business Angels to see their service or product offering, as well as providing the opportunity to network with these Entrepreneurs and other Business Angels. A potential Business Angel can always join other Angel networks around their country if finding these a good source of opportunities.

London Business Angels (LBA)

London Business Angels is a Business Angel network that has been operational for approximately thirty years. LBA is supported by a number of advisory companies and promotes early stage companies in the South of England and through NESTA has links with other regional Business Angel networks. NESTA is now holding speed-networking meetings where Business Angels, Entrepreneurs, Venture Capital and professional advisors are provided with a platform to meet together at one event.

The LBA holds Angel Investor meetings, approximately eight times a year, where up to six Entrepreneurs will professionally present their proposition to tight deadlines and answer questions from the floor, all over a couple of hours, as well as an opportunity to network with the Entrepreneurs and other Business Angels. In addition, they also hold educational seminars for Entrepreneurs looking for Angel investment and potential Angel Investors, at which there will also be professional advisors that can be networked with.

LBA review many proposals from Entrepreneurs seeking Angel investment, but only a few are selected to present to their Business Angel network and will usually be the better opportunities. You will see how many executive summaries are reviewed and how few are actually selected to present at these meetings from the most recent statistics in chapter 9.

LBA review many investment opportunities, few are selected to present to their Business Angels

This is an annual fee paying membership (£295 plus VAT for 2011) and I also recommend that the potential Business Angel join this organization, as one of the most professional, to access these presentations and the benefit they will receive from networking with other active Business Angels.

LBA has also developed and manage several EIS funds in which some of their Angel Investor members have invested. These EIS funds, having the right in the LBA's contract with the Entrepreneur, then may invest alongside the Angel Investor or Syndicate who are investing directly in the Entrepreneur's business.

Beer & Associates

This is a professional, commercial organization that has a group of regional executives around the UK, sourcing early stage business investment opportunities. It also helps the Entrepreneurs develop their presentations, executive summary and ready them to meet with their extensive list of Angel investors.

There are no membership fees to be added to their investor list

They hold large Angel investor meetings in London twice a year at which as many as thirty Entrepreneurs present their investment propositions on a face-to-face basis with interested Business Angels. They also hold smaller regional investor meetings and provide weekly and add hoc email circulars to their list of Angel investors depending on their business sector interests.

Beer & Associates has developed several property funds for their Angel Investor members to invest in, but as property is not eligible for the benefits of EIS, this is of no interest of Angel Investors whose priority is to invest in EIS eligible businesses.

AngelNews

Modwenna Rees-Mogg publishes an online newsletter called "AngelNews" available on **www.AngelNews.co.uk.**, which include SME job opportunities, general articles on investing, conferences, government grants, AngelNews events, the general economic environment for Business Angels and listing companies looking for Angel investment.

A must for future Business Angels researching the Business Angel market

Other Angel Investor Websites

There are many websites such as **www.AngelInvestmentNetwork. co.uk** for the UK, **www.AngelsDen.co.uk**, **www.highgateTechFund. com** that is specifically focused on high tech opportunities, **www. advantagebusinessangels.com**, a Midlands based network, and **www.companypartners.com** that contains a lot of information before an Entrepreneur or Business Angel looks for opportunities.

For ease of reference, I have listed the UK Business Angel networks at the end of this book.

CHAPTER THREE

What information do Business Angels initially review?

This is not an exhaustive list of what Business Angels look for, which will vary depending upon the interest of the individual Angel, but these are areas that should be looked at, to both understand the business and the risk.

Type of Opportunity

Most Business Angels will be fairly specific about what type of businesses they are interested by and willing to invest in. While one should have an open mind and see as many opportunities as possible, so as not to "throw out the bath with the bath water", this is the stage that a Business Angel will decide to give a potential opportunity some time.

I will personally not look at all at pharmaceutical/biotech/ medical equipment/agricultural as they require far too long to bring to the market and require numerous fund raising rounds, nor film finance as it is prone to the fickle public making it very high risk, nor beer/wine/liquour/soft drink opportunities where there is fierce competition from the major suppliers and often very poor margins after marketing and distribution costs.

Executive Summary

Professional two page Executive Summary outlining the business, market, management experience, amount of and how the funding is to be used, performance history to date (if applicable), three year outlook after investment and most likely exit strategy.

Understanding the Basic Business Model

The business model of the service or product and it's ability to be flexed, needs to be understood in terms of sale price options, cost of sale and gross margin per service or product, and how many sales are needed to cover the overhead before being profitable.

In my experience, the business model outline
is often missing from the Executive Summary,
although essential to understanding how
the business can be geared up

Existing management

Meet the management team to assess them for personality, enthusiasm, experience, track record and whether the Business Angel believes he can develop a good working relationship with them. In addition, given the type of business, what management skills are missing, which are often one of sales, marketing, PR or financial experience, and assess whether the Business Angel can contribute to these missing skills. If skills need to be recruited in the future, make sure the cost is included in the forward projections.

While we all encourage youngsters to start their own businesses, most winners are actually in their 30's and 40's by the time they succeed, as prior business experience counts.

Idea, market potential and competition

Review the business competitive edge or unique selling point, the characteristics, competition and growth potential of the market in the country of operation, and whether this could have international market appeal.

Financial commitment of the Entrepreneur

What financial commitment has the Entrepreneur made? Has the Entrepreneur put in some of their money, given up a good job, and how long and professionally has the Entrepreneur spent on proving the product/service/concept?

IP or Copyright protection

Does the business have appropriate copyright protection over its brand name, logo and intellectual property, and is it in the name of the company or held directly by the Entrepreneur?

Operating and Administrative Location

This is important if the Business Angel wishes to be in regular contact with the Entrepreneur, and be able to easily make unannounced visits to enable them to see what is actually happening in the business. After my own personal experience of investing in businesses both in my locality and further afield, I will now only invest in my own locality.

Is it a Start-Up?

If it is a start-up with, for example, a website to be developed or under development and no real proven business model, this will be a much higher risk than an early stage business that has contracts and/or a limited proven revenue stream. Valuation becomes more difficult in the case of a start-up, particularly if there are really no other similar offerings in the market place.

Is it an Individual, Partnership or Company?

If the business is in the form of an individual or partnership, the Business Angel will almost certainly wish the Entrepreneur to register the business as a company as a form of protection for the Angel investor against future risk of liability should the business fail. In this unfortunate position, this also has tax implications, as the Business Angel will want to crystallize any capital loss to be able to offset against any capital gains from other investments.

Is it a Syndicate Funding?

If the Entrepreneur wants a group of small investors, then one of the Angel networks will be always the best way to go about raising the funds required. I personally prefer to avoid Syndicate funding and complete the full funding so that I may have more influence in the development of the business.

Is it a Life Style Business?

A Life Style Business is one where the Entrepreneur desires to generate a high profile for themselves ahead of the real development of the business, becoming satisfied when they have reached a level of profitability that matches their remuneration and benefits expectation.

I personally now avoid life style businesses, as I have had a bad experience of such a business, where if the ambition had been there, the business would have in the future, had the ability to form an international franchise in major cities of the World, which was not to be.

Shareholder Structure

It is important to understand the existing shareholder structure at what valuation those shareholders have invested (if any), as this may affect how the Business Angel(s) will fit into this existing shareholder base.

I personally now avoid investing in businesses that have multiple shareholders and it is amazing how many Entrepreneurs have poorly managed this with a mish mash of early stage small investors, no doubt in their urgency to raise funding. I personally now only look for a clean share register in which only the direct Founder(s) are shareholders and with whom I can have a common understanding relating to the development of the company.

However, I do encourage the Founder(s) to grant shares and/ or share options to the early management so that they may benefit from their hard work towards the future success of the company. In the UK, the company can register a share option scheme with the HMRC, that is tax beneficial by avoiding any tax being payable on the grant of the share options, otherwise the recipients would have to pay income tax on the value of the shares when granted.

Business Angels should encourage the Entrepreneur to grant shares/share options to management

While this is dilutive for the Founder and Business Angels' equity, they will normally more than reap the benefit by keeping a dedicated management team and minimize the disruption and cost of replacing management.

Funding Amount Required

Amount of funding requested and timing – is it to be invested in tranches?

Proposed Percentage of Equity

The number of shares to be issued and percentage of the increased total equity that places a specific valuation on the business. The valuation of start-ups and early stage businesses is really an art rather than a science and prior business experience will help the Business Angel assess this.

Early stage business valuation
is an art, not a science!

As I personally wish to be the sole Angel investor, I believe that taking 30% of the equity is equitable and a fair alignment with the Entrepreneur given my own skills and experience. Fortunately, this also falls into line with the maximum permitted under the UK's tax beneficial Enterprise Investment Scheme ("EIS") and the potential Business Angel Seed Investment Scheme ("BASIS") to be operational in April 2012, which are both referred to in more detail in chapter 5.

I know other Business Angels who expect the Entrepreneur to give them 51% of the shares for being the sole Angel investor as they wish to have ultimate control, but I believe this is a disincentive for the Entrepreneur. However, the Shareholder Agreement can minimize most risks of not having a controlling shareholding, by having clauses that require the Entrepreneur to have prior agreement from the shareholders for specific matters that are referred to in chapter 6. Alternatively, an option could be for the Shareholder Agreement to have a clause enabling the Founder to have an exit ratchet, on the future sale of the company to compensate them not having control and benefit on the success of the company.

At this initial review stage, I would not recommend that the Business Angel gets into any discussion relating to valuation but just note what the expectation of the Entrepreneur is. Once the Business Angel has completed their due diligence noted in chapter 5, they will have to decide whether to invest, having formed an opinion as to the reasonableness of the Entrepreneurs valuation, and this is the time to negotiate any amendment to that expectation.

*The Business Angel should establish the
Entrepreneur's valuation expectations,
but not negotiate at this stage*

Business Angel Review Checklist

Investment Opportunity	1	2	3	4	5
Opportunity Type					
Executive Summary					
Basic Business Model					
Existing Management					
Idea, Market Potential & Competition					
Entrepreneur's Financial Commitment					
IP & Copyright Protection					
Operating & Administrative Location					
Start-up or Early Stage					
Individual, Partnership or Company					
Syndicate or One Investor					
Is it a Life Style Business					
Shareholder Structure					
Funding Required					
Proposed Equity Percentage (Valuation)					
Grand Total					

Score each category from 1 for low quality to 10 for high quality –
avoid scores under 80%.

Comments:

_____

_____

_____

_____

_____

_____

_____

_____

_____

_____

_____

_____

CHAPTER FOUR

What should an Entrepreneur look for in a Business Angel?

Ultimately, the Entrepreneur must ensure that the Business Angel(s) willing to invest in them are right for the business and the paragraphs below reflect an example of where this went wrong with one of my own investments.

The husband of a lady, whom I had known for a couple of years, asked me if I would help by providing seed capital and provide support to his wife who was setting up a business. The amount was relatively small, I liked the concept and I agreed to invest. One of the conditions of the investment was that we meet weekly and that I would provide advice and support, which I fulfilled.

However, after approximately six months, the meetings became less frequent due to the apparent lack of availability of the Entrepreneur. This was after she became unhappy with a second round funding proposal that included introducing another Business Angel to invest alongside myself. I finally established from her husband, that this was because she felt that she could progress her business without these consultations and felt she was wasting her time.

To be fair to this lady, she bought out my investment, and the business is still operational several years later. This business has not developed into the size it could have, but ultimately this was her life style choice. In hindsight, our visions for the future of the business did not appear to match, despite having expressed to her that the business could be developed in major cities of the world through creating a franchise model.

Compatibility of Entrepreneur and Business Angel

It is important that the management team and a sole Business Angel or Lead Investor are compatible, have a common vision for the development of the business rather than noted above, and will be able to work together for the mutual benefit of both parties.

The Angel Investor and Entrepreneur should have a common vision for the business's development

The Entrepreneur needs to assess this not only when accepting to allow due diligence to proceed with a specific Business Angel, but also during due diligence and the negotiation of the Shareholder Agreement. While it may be frustrating to decide to stop the potential transaction, life could become a lot more difficult later if the parties fall out and the progress of the development of business is delayed, and in a worse case scenario, a lot of time wasting and legal costs.

Advice and Encouragement

The Entrepreneur should look for advice and encouragement from the Business Angel. While an investor simply demands a financial return, an Angel should encourage the Entrepreneur to build a successful business, roll up their sleeves to help when necessary, and help with fresh ideas or solutions rather than complain when something goes wrong.

Business Angel Skills

It is important that the Business Angel's skills match the needs of the business, particularly if the Business Angel or Lead Investor wants some active involvement, in which case the Entrepreneur needs to ensure the Business Angel or Lead Investor can add some value though their past experience and business contacts.

The Entrepreneurs should do their own due diligence on the Business Angel or Lead Investor. As Samuel Johnson put it: "almost every man wastes part of his life in attempts to display qualities which he does not possess, and to gain applause which he cannot keep".

The ideal fit is where a Business Angel has really good previous business experience of both large business disciplines and small business development, strategy, acquiring and disposing of businesses, funding and if available an additional benefit of having listed companies on Plus and/or AIM. This will allow the Business Angel to be able to give good advice gained from previous experience, and as the business grows, to help to obtain additional capital, and possibly the acquisition of other businesses where appropriate.

In addition, from this range of experience, the Entrepreneur will have the knowledgeable support of their Business Angel at the time of reviewing the exit strategy of a trade sale or an IPO, and help to execute this. This means the Angel Investor is capable of helping the Entrepreneur through the full life cycle of the business to exit.

Single Business Angel or a Syndicate

The Entrepreneur needs to assess whether they wish to have a single Business Angel or a Lead Investor for a Syndicate, which may also affect the Entrepreneur's decision as to where to search for suitable investors. A lot will depend on how urgent raising funds are and it may be that within the Business Angel networks that there may be a Business Angel willing and able to be a sole investor.

Future financial ability of the Business Angel

The Entrepreneur should assess the financial ability of the Business Angel(s) to contribute to future funding rounds as typically this will be required two or three times before the exit. I am amazed, that I have never been asked this question by an "Entrepreneur". I assume the priority and urgency of funding over rides this!

Never asked by an Entrepreneur if I can fund future funding rounds!

As I prefer to be the sole Business Angel, I always make sure the Entrepreneur understands my ability to support future funding as this is an advantage over Syndicates, where there are bound to be some Business Angels not willing to participate in second and third funding rounds.

In a worst case scenario, where none of the Angel Investors are willing to enter a second or third round of investment, this can make it difficult to find other Business Angels willing to invest because of the inevitable question, "why are your current investors not contributing?"

A potential risk of failing if unable to secure additional funds

Business Angel Accessibility

Particularly where the Business Angel wishes to be close to the business as a Non Executive Director, the Entrepreneur should assess whether the Business Angel has realistic availability to support the business management team. In other words, what other commitments does the Business Angel have, such as a full time job or being a frequent traveller, that may limit their availability.

To quote an American Entrepreneur, Winton G. Rossiter (MBA Harvard Business School) and founder of JazzyMedia and Weight Wins:

"A good Business Angel is like a demanding parent, an investor is more of a lazy banker!"

Non Disclosure Agreement ("NDA")

Lastly, but very importantly, the Entrepreneur must ensure that they obtain a signature from a sole Angel Investor or Lead Investor on an NDA before they start their due diligence. The Entrepreneur should have his solicitor draw up a suitable NDA to protect the Entrepreneur should they take the business idea to somebody else to develop. This provides the protection of legal recourse should this happen, but the best protection is to take references and make enquiries as to the honesty and reliability of the potential investor(s).

Entrepreneur's View of Business Angel Attributes Check List

Business Angels being considered	1	2	3	4	5
Compatibility with Angel or Lead Investor					
Perceived Advice & Encouragement Ability					
Business Angel Skills					
Single Business Angel or Syndicate					
Financial Ability of Angel/Lead Investor					
Business Angel/Lead Investor Availability					
Grand Total					

Score each category from 1 for low quality to 10 for high quality – avoid scores under 80%.

Comments:

_____

_____

_____

_____

_____

_____

_____

_____

_____

_____

_____

_____

CHAPTER FIVE

What is the next step for the Business Angel?

There will probably be a substantial amount of "Due Diligence" that the Business Angel will wish to do, particularly if the business has been developing for some time. I personally find that it is during the due diligence process and the eventual negotiation of the Shareholder Agreement that one discovers whether this is really a business one wishes to invest in and just as importantly, that the relationships are likely to work in the future.

Where the Business Angel has limited business experience, it may well be appropriate to appoint a solicitor and a small firm of accountants to carry out the due diligence.

The headings of the likely due diligence information that the Business Angel should request and what to look for are noted below. This is not an exhaustive list, nor in any order of priority, and will vary depending upon the company's stage of development, market and type of business.

Past financial performance

What revenue has been achieved (if any) and what expenditure has been incurred to date, how much remuneration has the

Entrepreneur(s) paid themselves, if any, and what unsettled past liabilities are there to be paid off after funds have been raised?

Future Business Plan

There should be a reasonably documented business plan detailing the market, competition and strategic steps to be taken over the next three years. If this is not available, meetings need to be held to thrash out the planned direction of the business and document this detail.

Future financial performance projections

There should be detailed monthly projections over three years and the Business Angel should assess the likelihood of the revenue being achieved and review the adequacy of the overhead costs. In my experience, the original projections are never achieved and when I invest I usually ask the Entrepreneur to scale back the business projections, as I prefer to incentivize the management to over achieve. This gives the business a more positive operational environment, presuming of course they do meet these lowered expectations!

I often see Executive Summaries and business plans projected over five years, I assume to justify the valuation through these projections. I personally, only look at the first three years, as I do not believe early stage companies can realistically project so far out in such a fast moving world.

How proposed funds are to be spent

Review how the funds, once received, are to be spent and over what timeframe, and the likelihood of a second or third funding round. In addition, you should reach agreement as to the review of this spending with the Entrepreneur on a regular basis and agree contract and capital expenditure approval procedures above a certain level that requires the Business Angels agreement.

Level of Management Salary Expectation

Review the salary levels projected in the Business Plan for reasonableness and annual growth. In the UK, I believe the Entrepreneur as Chief Executive Officer, of an early stage business, should be permitted to earn approximately £35,000 to £50,000 per annum in London, with the ability to earn a bonus based on over achieving the reduced projections referred to above. This salary level should not be increased until the business is cash flow positive and on a firm footing.

I personally will not progress any investment where I find the Entrepreneur has excessive salary expectations. This is in the Entrepreneur's interest as more funds are kept in the business and are available for safe growth, as well as increasing the value of the business for all shareholders, including themselves.

Accounting Systems and Administration

Assess what computer and accounting systems are being used, the management of other administrative needs, the quality and experience of the accounting and administrative personnel, and consider if additional resources or accounting systems upgrades may be required.

Intellectual Property ("IP")

Inspect documentation confirming IP rights to copyrights, logo's, patents and any other intellectual property are secured. This should also include internet domain name registration agreements.

Articles of Association and Company Registration Documents

The company's Articles of Association need to be reviewed to confirm that the company has authority to operate in the relevant business sector, details of the shareholder voting rights, pre-emption rights, etc. The Articles should be revised in line with the new Shareholder Agreement so that they are properly aligned.

In addition, inspect the company registration documents since formation of the company where there have been one or more name changes since formation.

Previous Board Meeting Minutes

These need to be reviewed from the company's formation for past activity and Board approvals, including the authority for any previous fund raising and to raise the proposed additional capital from Angel Investors. In most cases, depending upon the stage of the company's development, the Board meeting minutes are likely to be very limited for early stage companies.

Potential for Future Funding

The Shareholder Agreement should clearly state the basis upon which future fund raising can be carried out and usually the authorization required of the Business Angel(s), who should always have the right of first refusal on future funding rounds known as "pre-emption rights". As mentioned above, Angel Investors should expect to be requested to provide additional funds two or three times after the initial funding.

Likely Exit Opportunity and Timing

The Entrepreneur should have a view of the most likely exit outcome, trade sale or IPO, and timing for the Angel Investor depending on the business sector, although this is difficult to assess for an early stage company. Ideally this should be between three years and certainly no longer than five years from investment, although it can often be much longer.

*Business Angels should expect
to be invested for five years*

One Business Angel I know advised me that one of his successful investments was in a company he had invested in twelve years ago and had recently become an AIM listed company. I personally wish to be able to exit by the end of five years.

UK Tax Considerations

An Angel Investor should consider his/her personal tax position now and in the future, as well as the tax position of the company, and should seek professional tax advice before making any investment.

As part of the UK Budget's "Plan for Growth" the Treasury increased the benefits of the Enterprise Investment Scheme ("EIS") in the April 2011 Budget and proposed a new Business Angel Seed Investment Scheme ("BASIS") to generate more "seed" funding for companies at the pre-trading stage, but this is unlikely to be operational before April 2012. Details of the UK tax beneficial schemes are detailed below, as they can be very valuable to Business Angels in boosting future potential returns.

Enterprise Investment Scheme ("EIS")

Has the company registered for the EIS scheme and can the Angel Investor take advantage of this UK beneficial tax scheme for early stage businesses? The Business Angel will have to decide whether they want their equity stake to be over 30% of the issued capital for the funds they are providing and/or being actively involved in the day to day business in the early years, as restrictions on these would result in their being unable to take the benefit of this scheme. However, there is a concession that a Business Angel may be an initially unpaid Non Executive Director ("NED"), but can become a paid NED later in the development of the business. There are also anti-avoidance rules that restrict the investor from making loans to the company as a way of keeping the equity at or below 30%.

It should also be noted that companies dealing in commodities, financial instruments, banking, hiring, legal, accountancy, property development, farming, timber, coal, steel, hotels and nursing homes are excluded from the EIS Scheme. In addition, EIS is only available on unquoted companies with gross assets of up to £15m, no more than 250 full-time employees and raising no more than £10m via the EIS scheme in twelve months. The annual investment limit is currently £500,000 and is due to rise to £1m from April 2012.

One of the tax benefits of the EIS scheme is, that there is relief of 20% of the cost of the investment up to a maximum of £100,000 in 2011 and £200,000 from April 2012 (£500,000 investment in 2011 and £1m investment from April 2012) that may be set against the Angels income tax liability in the year the investment is made, provided the Angel has sufficient income tax liability to cover it.

There is also a "carry back" facility that allows all or part of this 20% of the cost of the shares acquired in any one tax-year, to be treated as though the shares had been acquired in the preceding tax year. This excludes set off against dividend income, as the tax credit attached to the dividend is not recoverable. In order to benefit from this concession, the shares must be held for three years or otherwise HMRC will recover the benefit received.

In addition, there is no Capital Gains Tax on the sale of shares or one can defer any previous year capital gains tax up to the maximum £500,000 (or £1m in 2012). The investment is also inheritance tax-free after two years under the Business Property Relief. The minimum holding period is three years in order to benefit from the other tax concessions.

Loss relief can be obtained where the shares are disposed of at a loss, which may be set against income in the year in which the shares were disposed of, less any income tax relief previously given on the initial investment.

This is a very important tax saving opportunity, worth exploring and considering while the Business Angel is structuring the deal. It is also quite complex and is worth taking professional tax advice if you have not made use of these concessions before. You can obtain a reasonable outline from the HMRC website **www.hmrc.gov.uk/eis.**

EIS is an important tax concession
available to Business Angels

Business Angel Seed Investment Scheme ("BASIS")

The UK government has issued a consultation document proposing a new scheme called BASIS which is expected to be completed by the end of September 2011, to be amended for announcement in the 2012/13 Budget. The current proposal is that the scheme would cover wealthy private individuals, who invest directly in new unquoted businesses but do not have more than a 30% stake in companies that are at a "pre-trading" stage. The proposal is that Business Angels investing in companies already trading would not be eligible, but the definition of what "pre-trading" is has not yet been established.

The proposed BASIS scheme's tax benefits being considered appear to be similar to the EIS scheme but we will have to wait for the scheme to be passed into the tax law before we can be certain of the benefits.

UK Corporation Tax

If the business looking for investment has actually been trading, you should assess if any corporation tax is payable and/or overdue for payment, in the unlikely event that the business is profitable. The Business Angel should also establish whether there have been any HMRC inspections and the outcome and any penalties.

It is more probable that there will be accumulated tax losses, and what tax benefit there will be from prior trading losses that will benefit the company, being off settable against profits, once the company starts making profits. This will obviously be beneficial to the company's future cash flow.

Payroll Taxes

The Angel Investor should establish that all payroll taxes (Pay as you Earn and National Insurance in the UK) have been paid on a timely basis, that all monthly and annual returns required have been filed, and that there have been no HMRC inspections and if so, details of the outcome and any penalties.

Value Added Taxes ("VAT")

The Angel Investor should establish whether the company is registered for VAT, and if not that any revenue is below the VAT registration threshold that requires the company to be registered. If the company is VAT registered, what VAT payment scheme is it being operated under, have VAT payments been made on a timely basis, has there been a VAT inspection and if so, details of the outcome and any penalties.

Overseas Taxation

Other countries have similar tax regulations that should be considered as part of the whole investment opportunity if the Angel Investor is non-resident in the country the company is registered in.

What Value can the Business Angel add?

Some Angel Investors do not want to be involved in any way in the business and this may well be the reason why so many wish to be part of a Syndicate, investing small sums in multiple businesses. However, a sole Angel Investor will almost definitely wish to be close to the ongoing business and the Entrepreneur needs to decide what limits, if any, they want to place on this.

Most Angel Investor providing all the funds will wish to be close to the business

As a sole investor in a business, I would personally want to be close to the ongoing business with initial weekly meeting, later reduced to two weekly meetings. In addition, I would want to be a modestly paid Non Executive Director when allowed to under the EIS or BASIS schemes, and be able to add value through mentoring and working my contacts from my past business experience.

Contracts

Review all existing contracts and any heads of terms relating to potential new contracts. This should include employee contracts, supplier contracts, supply fulfillment contracts, credit card agreements, banking arrangements, and membership contracts where appropriate.

Insurance Cover

Review and inspect all insurance policies, which should include employee liability, motor, building and contents as appropriate, and other legal protection policies.

Other Legal Requirements

Data Protection Act registration and make sure the company is abiding by the Money Laundering Regulations and has the necessary procedures where the amounts of the transactions require this.

Gut Feeling

Ultimately, after all the above due diligence, a belief there is a good business case and a fair chance of success, my last criteria is a good "Gut Feeling" about the business proposition and the management team. Does the management team have the energy, enthusiasm and skill set to achieve?

Business Angel Due Diligence Check List

Investment Opportunity	1	2	3	4	5
Past Financial Performance					
Quality of Accounting & Administration					
Future Business Plan & Projections					
How Funds Invested to be Spent					
Management Salary Expectations					
Non Disclosure Agreement					
Intellectual Property					
Articles of Association					
Previous Board Meeting Minutes					
Potential for Future Funding					
Likely Exit Opportunity & Timing					
EIS and/or BASIS Availability					
UK Corporation Tax Position & Inspections					
Payroll Taxes/NI & Inspections					
VAT & Inspections					
Any Overseas Taxation Issues					
Ability to Add Value to Entrepreneur					
Gut Feeling!					
Contracts					
Company Policy Documents					
Quality of Website					
Grand Total					

Score each category from 1 for low quality to 10 for high quality – avoid scores under 80%.

Comments:

_____

_____

_____

_____

_____

_____

_____

_____

_____

_____

_____

_____

CHAPTER SIX

What should the Shareholder Agreement contain?

The Shareholder Agreement, or alternatively named the Investment Agreement, will normally be produced by the Entrepreneur's lawyer and the Angel Investor should use the advice of their own lawyer unless having previous experience of this. The headings below are the typical clauses you are likely to find in a UK Shareholder Agreement and in addition there will be the usual boilerplate clauses.

One thing the Entrepreneur should consider in the case of a Syndicate investment, is that any future changes to the Articles and/ or the Shareholder Agreement will require every investor to sign the documentation, which can be administratively burdensome and costly for the company.

Change to Articles of Association (Articles)

The Shareholder Agreement should have the Articles as an appendix to the Agreement. Modifications to the Articles will almost certainly require to be made to reflect the details agreed in the Shareholder Agreement and the Angel Investor must makes sure matters referred to below are included where appropriate.

Description of the Business

This will outline the business, principal objectives and any copyrights, patents or other intellectual property held.

Description of relationship with Entrepreneur

Minimum number of Board meetings each year, any other mandatory meetings agreed, etc.

Investment to be made and number of shares to be issued (Subscription)

This is a list of the new shareholder names, number of shares and amount subscribed by each, details of multiple subscriptions to be made (if any) and warranties given by the company and between each of the company and the new shareholders.

The Angel Investor should also make sure that the Shareholder Agreement and Articles provide for the Angel Investor to have pre-emption rights, whereby the Angel Investor has the right to invest in further equity when the Board wishes to raise further funding and other investors participate.

Completion

This lays out the process when and how payment is to be made and what the company's obligations are at the time of completion, such as holding a board meeting to approve the issue of the equity, issuing share certificates, etc.

Warranties and Limitations

This is a clause stating the warranties that the company makes to the new shareholder(s) and the limitations to the level of warranties. It is normal that these warranties are only valid for the first twelve months following the investment and only become payable if any future claim is within this timeframe.

The warranty limits usually applying are, any amounts in excess of 10% of the investment for any single warranty claim, limited to a maximum of 100% of the funds invested for any accumulated number of warranty breaches. This is entirely negotiable between the parties and the Entrepreneur should consider his/her likely exposure.

The list of individual warranties is normally quite long and is normally included as an appendix to the Shareholder Agreement. The Business Angel will of course hope that they will never need to make a warranty claim and is merely a protection against their investment.

Board of Directors ("Board")

This clause states the appointment of the Angel Investor as a director, if applicable, the addition of any other person agreed to strengthen the Board and/or the dismissal of any director previously on the Board. This clause will also indicate the maximum number of directors on the Board, the frequency of Board meetings and the process for the Founders remuneration to be reviewed, and these matters should be mirrored in the revised Articles.

The directors should also be provided with employment contracts to be agreed and added as an appendix to the Shareholder Agreement. These must include a "good leaver – bad leaver" clause, that in essence provides for a procedure if their services are to be terminated under prescribed conditions and how their shareholding is to be dealt with if they wish to sell or the company wants to recover the shares if they are a "bad" leaver.

Accounting, Business Plan and Information Rights

This clause outlines the company's obligation to maintain accurate and complete accounting and financial records, the frequency and timing of reporting of management accounts, the timing of providing the annual accounts to the Board and whether they should be audited. It may also layout the timing and frequency of the updating of the business plan.

When I invest, I always demand that the annual accounts are audited and that this is included in the above clause. In general, unless the business is unduly complex, the early years audit fees will be relatively small compared to the later benefit.

Always insist that the company's future
annual accounts are audited

The reason for insisting the annual accounts are audited, besides promoting a professional approach, is that additional funding from a Venture Capital firm and/or obtaining a bank loan will be made easier and faster. In addition, after a few years, when it comes to negotiating a trade sale or pursuing an IPO, it makes due diligence so much easier and shows a professional approach to running the company. It is also a safety net for the Business Angel in the unlikely event of fraud or wrong doing by the management team.

Matters requiring Investor consent

This is a clause where the company undertakes not to amend the Articles, create, allot, issue any shares or securities or vary the voting rights or grant any share options, not to acquire any other business, not to sign contracts in excess of say twelve months as appropriate, not to employ any person with a salary over a certain amount (usually in the region of £25,000 per annum) nor with a notice period in excess of a certain time period (normally 3 months) without agreement of the Board of directors, not to declare or pay dividends, nor make loans to Directors and only to enter into contracts or agreements on an arm's length basis.

It is often appropriate to add a clause that requires the Angel Investor(s) to approve all contracts in excess of say twelve months and/or an agreed value amount, or as appropriate, capital expenditure in excess of an agreed level, any future employees appointments over the agreed limits on remuneration and notice periods, and any future salary increases.

Promotion of the Company's Business

This clause outlines the responsibility of the Founders and Angel Investor(s) to promote the best interests of the business, use the funds subscribed in furtherance of the business and to take such actions as are required to protect the IP rights, the Shareholder Agreement and the Articles.

Transfer of Shares

The Founders agree not to create an encumbrance over or transfer any of their shares to another party without the consent of the Board, which normally requires unanimous consent. Normally transfers of shares between spouses are acceptable and this is also allowed under the EIS scheme.

Event of Exit

This clause covers the process required to be carried out by the Board should the company be approached with an offer to buy the company and what happens in the event of any dispute or disagreement.

This clause should also include "tag along" rights, whereby the Angel Investor(s) also have automatic rights to sell their shares on the same terms and conditions as the Founder.

Effect of ceasing to hold shares

This covers the event that the Founder should cease to hold his shares, be a Director and employee of the company.

Restrictive covenants

This clause restricts the Founders and Directors from engaging in or being interested in a business competing with the company and for a period (normally between 6 and 12 months depending upon the likely business risk) after they cease to be a director or employee, and not to carry on or be interested in a similar business. This will also include a clause not to entice away any of the company's employees or have any dealings with the company's clients, customers, suppliers, agents or distributors for an agreed period (normally 12 months).

Confidentiality and Announcements

This clause requires the Founders and the company not to make any announcements about the Shareholder Agreement without prior approval of the Angel Investor(s) and the Board other than required by law and/or regulatory or government requirements.

Assignment

This normally restricts any of the shareholders from assigning rights, transferring or delegating any of their obligations under the Shareholder Agreement without agreement of the other shareholders in writing.

Shareholder Obligations

This clause requires each shareholder to exercise all voting rights and other powers of control over the company at all times during the time the Shareholder Agreement remains valid. It will also state that if there is any conflict with the Articles, this clause will prevail between the parties.

Severance

This clause generally states that if any clause in the Shareholder Agreement is to be found to be invalid, unenforceable or illegal by any court, then all the other provisions in the Shareholder Agreement will remain in force.

Variation

This clause states that any variations to the Shareholder Agreement are only valid if in writing and signed by all the parties to it.

Costs

This clause usually states the company is responsible for the costs associated with the Shareholder Agreement or alternatively, each party (the company and the Angel Investors) is responsible for their own costs.

As an Angel Investor, I would expect the company to bear all of the costs as I generally will review the Shareholder Agreement myself and ask for appropriate amendments. If the Angel Investor has not done this before they should use a lawyer to protect their interests and pay their own costs.

Whole Agreement

This clause generally states that this Shareholder Agreement and appendices are the final agreement and that any prior understandings, arrangements or agreements are covered by the agreement.

Notices

This clause outlines where and how any notices to the company should be directed.

Governing Law and Jurisdiction

This will generally be the country in which the company is registered. In the unusual circumstances where the Entrepreneur, tries to demand jurisdiction be in his country of residence, the Entrepreneur should avoid this at all costs. It could turn out to be both time consuming for the company and very costly, should there be a dispute in the future requiring legal support.

Insurance Cover

Depending on the type of business, you may wish to have written into the Shareholder Agreement an obligation for the company to insure against specific events, as well as the mandatory insurance required by UK law.

Keyman Insurance

Specifically, I would recommend that the Angel Investor(s) demand the company take out a "Keyman" insurance policy on the Founding directors. In my view, this is essential where there is one Founder and no other experienced management team.

This provides a lump sum, in the unfortunate situation where the Founder or named directors die or are severely incapacitated, and allows the business to have additional funds to cover the costs of immediately inserting interim management and recruiting permanent executives.

Directors and Officers Insurance ("D&O")

In addition, the Angel Investor(s) may insist that the company takes out a D&O insurance policy to cover all directors, particularly if the sole Business Angel or Lead Investor becomes a director. This is only required where the company is planning for another round of funding and wishes to protect the existing directors in the event of a future claim.

As a member of the Institute of Directors, Hiscox Insurance offer a number of business insurance policies including a D&O policy on a discounted basis, but most brokers will be able to obtain cover for a relatively low cost. To explore the Hiscox offer, contact them on 0845 213 8901 or visit **www.iod.com/businessinsurance.**

Angel Protection Insurance

The privately owned, Lark Insurance Broking Group, have recently announced a new Angel Protection Insurance policy underwritten by QBE Insurance (Europe) Limited, Plantation Place, 30 Fenchurch Street, London EC3M 3BD. This protects Business Angels from numerous potential litigation risks while being a non executive director, or being considered as a shadow director on the basis of having influence as an investor over the business, even if not formally a director. To explore this, contact Nick Burrows, Lark Insurance Broking Group at direct line: 01206 771280, mobile: 07855 383682 and email: **Nick.Burrows@Larkinsurance.co.uk.**

CHAPTER SEVEN

How does the Angel Investor achieve an exit?

Unless the business proves to be successful, the Angel investor is highly unlikely to get their money back.

A successful business in a good growth market really has two options, depending upon its stage of development and the general economic climate, a "Trade" sale or a "Listing" on Plus or AIM. Details relating to Plus and AIM are referred to in chapter 1.

A trade sale is probably the easiest, less risky and fastest way to release value for the shareholders. In order to achieve the best price for the shares, it is preferable to appoint a professional advisor who knows the company's business sector and other companies who may be interested in the synergy of acquiring the business. Although, the Entrepreneur will obviously also have their own contacts with the management of other interested companies in the relevant business sector, who may be interested in buying the company, a professional advisor will add them to their list of their own contacts, and keep them at arms length during the auction process to ensure competition and market value is achieved.

The purchaser may well demand that the shareholders accept shares in the purchasing company, particularly if it is quoted on

AIM or the Main Market of the London Stock Exchange, or a combination of shares and cash. My personal advice is to avoid accepting any shares of the purchasing company, and only accept cash, as you have no control over the progress of the acquiring company and the quoted value of their shares can just as well fall after the acquisition.

In general, only accept cash
on the sale of the business

The other alternative of a listing on Plus or AIM, is much more costly and risky, because after completing the Prospectus and a great deal of expense, the condition of the financial markets and/or in your business sector can change suddenly and the listing can fail through no fault of the company.

If this happens, you have to bear all the advisor costs that in some cases might result in forcing the company into administration, particularly if further funding cannot be achieved quickly by other means. I have been in this position with other companies where at the last minute the listing could not be completed, or the offer price has to be reduced, because of an event outside the management's control and in one case, this nearly resulted in the company being put into administration.

CHAPTER EIGHT

What are the chances of a successful exit?

It is an often quoted rule of thumb, that an Angel Investor will only have one successful investment out of ten different investments and this may be the reason why so many of the Angel networks seem to have so many Syndicate Investors.

Only one in ten Angel investments is likely to be successful

My own approach is to try and provide the complete funding requirement, which rules out participating in many of the larger fund raisings (which can be perceived as a disadvantage), become a Non Executive Director and have regular meetings to support the management team. I personally feel this gives the Business Angel the best chance of being successful and it is also very rewarding.

Successful Investments

Out of four Angel investments I have made, despite looking at hundreds of Executive Summaries and attending Entrepreneur presentations, I have managed to exit one through a successful trade sale after 5 years, one where I have been bought out by the Founder with a small gain after 12 months due to disagreement over an additional funding proposal.

I have also recently made a sole Angel investment in Weight Wins, **www.weightwins.com.**

Unsuccessful Investments

The two other investments were a complete disaster. In one case, as a Syndicate investor within a small investment group, with the right to attend Board meetings, I left these meetings with an uncomfortable feeling. I did not like the answers we were receiving in terms of sales and marketing progress, and management accounts were not being regularly prepared. This company was not in my locality and given these uncomfortable feelings, it was very inconvenient to just turn up and see what was actually going on.

Later the money ran out and I declined to make a further investment on the next funding round. Somebody the Founder personally knew provided a large investment of £250,000 and well in excess of the original Syndicate investment, to see himself loose all his money a couple of years later when the company failed.

*There is a lot to be said for acting
on your gut feelings!*

In the other case, I, and another retired Chartered Accountant, loaned money to a professional operator, whom I had met before, to acquire a single unit business within a large catchment area. On an unpaid basis, I became directly involved in the transfer of IT systems and setting up the monthly accounting systems, to ensure the regular production of monthly management accounts.

The business was very tightly "Bootstrapped" and we managed to get advance payments for services from a large company that the operator spent on a cosmetic refurbishment. However, the business continued to loose clients, and it was becoming harder and harder to replace them with new clients.

My view was that despite the professional operators previous claims of experience turning around other businesses of the same type, his approach to selling and marketing was not working, and the local catchment appeared unwilling to pay at a rate at which this business could be viable.

I was unwilling to inject any further capital into the business following my own assessment, and it became clear that my co-investor was also unwilling, resulting in myself and the other investor loosing all our money. Fortunately, the business was handed over to the company that had made the advanced payments for services, neatly avoiding us having to put the business into Administration.

One real success out of four investments is better than the average, but this is a high risk – high reward method of investing and is not for the weak hearted and any use of funds marked for retirement should not be risked!

High risk – high reward!

CHAPTER NINE

Business Angel investment statistics

There appears to be very little reliable international published Angel investment statistics. This is because investing in unquoted businesses is a private activity in an unorganized environment, lacking one access point and with no directories of Business Angels. The only visible market is made up of Angel networks and Angel Syndicates.

UK

The most up to date and only reliable data in the UK, has been produced for the second year running, in the "Annual Report on the Business Angel Market in the United Kingdom: 2009/10" produced by Professor Colin M. Mason of the Hunter Centre for Entrepreneurship, Strathclyde Business School, University of Strathclyde and Professor Richard T. Harrison of Queen's University Management School, Queen's University of Belfast.

The report was commissioned by a consortium led by the Department for Business, Innovation and Skills ("BIS") and comprising the Association of Chartered Certified Accountants ("ACCA"); the British Private Equity and Venture Capital Association

("BVCA"); and the Scottish Angel Capital Association ("LINC") and can be found on the BBAA website **www.bbaa.org.uk/research-policy/market-research.**

The BBAA data presented in this report is from their network members and is summarized below:

- *4,555 Angels at the end of 2009/10 compared with 5,548 Angels in 2008/09, an approximate 1,000 membership decline of 18%;*

- *fewer than 1,800 of their Angels were active, being 37% of the total;*

- *received 9,640 business plans in 2009/10, an increase of 11% on 2008/09;*

- *put forward 764 businesses to their investors, just 8% of all business plans received;*

- *presented 60 fewer business plans than in 2008/09;*

- *238 businesses raised finance in 2009/10, a marginal increase of 2% over 2008/09; and*

- *these companies raised £42.3m in 2009/10 compared with £44.9m in 2008/09, a decline of £2.6m or 6%;*

In addition to the BBAA, LINC Scotland reported 78 investments involving a total of £27.5m of which Business Angels contributed £18.2m or 66%. This indicates that UK Business Angels as a whole invested £60.5m in 2009/10, a decline of 3.7% compared with 2008/09. The professors' conclusion was that this reduction was due to the recession in 2009, following the financial crisis in 2008, which had curtailed Angels' exit opportunities and their capacity to recycle investment in new ventures.

The BBAA overall deal size ranges from £25,000 to over £1m but most deals are in the £50,000 to £500,000 range with fewer than 10% being £1m or more. Deal sizes were smaller in 2009/10 with 56% of investments under £200,000 compared with 48% in 2008/09.

Within the BBAA, in one-third of the deals Angels collectively invested less than £50,000 per deal, in over one-half of the deals Angels invested less than £100,000 and in three-quarters of the deals Angels invested less than £200,000. In addition, more than half of all investments involved at least two Angels and 18% involved more than five Angels.

Single Angel investors are more common where the investment is small and would seem to indicate these are Syndicate investors, start-ups or top-ups of previous investments. Individual Angels account for two-thirds of investments when the total investment is under £25,000. This proportion drops to 54% for investments between £25,000 and £49,000 and down to one-third when the amount invested is £50,000 or more.

Investments through the BBAA networks were mainly in early stage or start-up stage businesses but one-quarter of investments were in established companies looking for development capital. In relation to the size of these companies, over half were in companies with five or fewer employees and 78% had ten or fewer employees.

Angels investing through the BBAA networks invested 25% in IT/internet/software and telecoms, 19% in biotech/medical/healthcare and pharmaceutics, 12% in digital and creative industries, 11% in manufacturing, 10% in finance and business services with the remaining 23% in other sectors.

In a survey of 147 individual Business Angels, 67% were members of BBAA and 49% were members of Angel Syndicates. They collectively made 276 investments with 72% making at least one investment in 2009/10. The median made two investments and there was a small number making more than five investments. 56% of investors invested up to £50,000 in 2009/10 and 75% invested up to £100,000.

It is also interesting to note that 70% of these 147 Business Angels used the EIS scheme for at least some of their investments and 38% used EIS for all their investments. This indicates the importance of the governments EIS scheme supporting private investment into these early stage businesses.

On an adjusted basis, this report estimated that the overall scale of the Angel investment activity in the UK was approximately £317.7m in 2009/10 and suggested that the overall angel investment in the UK has declined 25% since 2008/09. This confirms the importance of Angel investing in supporting these early stage businesses, which is particularly important for the UK in the current economic climate and with the reluctance of banks to lend to small businesses.

In a separate study by NESTA (**www.nesta.org.uk**), it estimated that in 2009 there were between 4,000 and 6,000 Angel investors in the UK, which from the BBAA information above indicates that the majority of Angel investors are members of these Business Angel networks, with an average investment size of £42,000 per investment. This represented acquiring an average 8% of the equity of the venture and 10% of the equity of total investments accounting for more than 20% of the venture.

In terms of returns, 35% of investments produced returns of between one and five times the original investment, while 9% produced returns over ten times or more. The mean return was 2.2 times the investment in 3.6 years with an approximate internal rate return of 22% before tax. This compares with an expected 30% internal rate of return by venture capital firms.

Does this dispel the rule of thumb that one in ten Angel investments are successful?

Due to the fact that a large percentage of Angel investments are in businesses that fail, Angel investors should seek a return of at least 10 times their original investment within a 5 years period. However, ideally Business Angels should set their sights even higher, looking for businesses that have the potential to return between 20 and 30 times the original investment over a more realistic 5 to 7 year period.

The above UK statistics are rather out of date at the time of this publication and it does appear from attending both the LBA and Beer & Partners presentation days in the second quarter of 2011, that there are plenty of Business Angels actively looking for new opportunities – perhaps things are picking up again since this research. It could be that the low interest rates now and potentially over the next twelve months are encouraging private investors to seek capital gains to compensate.

USA

According to Wikipedia (**www.wikipedia.com**), in 2007 there was an Angel investment total of US$26 billion invested in 57,000 companies, or an average of US$450,000 per investment in the USA. This compares with USA Venture Capital investing US$30.69 billion in 3,918 companies, or an average of US$7.8m.

This really shows how much bigger the economy of the USA is over the UK detailed above. It also shows both how important Angel investment is to the growth of the US economy as well as the difference in magnitude between Angel and Venture Capital funding. The 2007 Angel investment was made up of 27% in software, 19% in healthcare services and medical devices and equipment, 12% in biotech and 42% across many other sectors.

The Centre for Venture Research (**www.unh.edu/news/ docs/2007AngelMarketAnalysis**) estimates that there were 258,000 active Angel Investors in the USA.

Canada

The 14 July 2011 AngelNews newsletter, details research carried out in Canada for the first time by the National Angel Capital Organization prepared by Professor Colin M. Mason of Strathclyde University, if any Business Angel wishes to research and invest in Canada. This market is relatively young with approximately half the Angel networks set up in the last three years.

There are three large networks, VANTEC, Angel Forum and Alberta Deal Generator that have over 200 members each and represent 58% of all Angel Investors and 55% of the completed deals. There are in total approximately 25 Angel networks, mainly focused on the country's main cities due to vast open areas of Canada, with approximately 1,500 Angel members.

CHAPTER TEN

An actual case study - successful exit

The case study below is an example of how a small business can produce an adequate return for a Business Angel. This was an investment that I actually made as the sole Angel Investor, as well as being very closely aligned to my view of the ideal opportunity discussed above, and a successful exit.

In 1999, I was lucky to find my first Angel investment through the London Business Angels network, which appears to have gone from strength to strength since then and that I have referred to in chapter 8.

I attended a London Business Angel presentation day at which the two New Zealander Founders of a company called UK Explorer Limited made a presentation and this generated a lot of interest from the attendees. I had a brief conversation with the two founders, who had stated in their presentation, that they were looking for a Syndicate funding as they had a small London based venture capital firm willing to co-invest with the Angel investors.

During this presentation and following a direct conversation with the Founders after the presentation, it became apparent to me, for reasons mentioned below, that I could be of great value to them. At this brief conversation, I indicated that for the right terms and satisfactory due diligence, that I would be willing to invest the whole amount they required of £300,000. I persuaded them the benefit was that there would be one negotiation and one person to deal with, rather than multiple Syndicate investors throughout the development of the business. I also believed that I could help add value strategically and had many contacts in the likely business arena that they would have to approach to develop their business.

Quite properly, they continued to talk to potential syndicate investors. However I had an exclusivity agreement for a limited period of time whilst I did my due diligence and we reached the stage of developing the Shareholder Agreement within this timeframe.

UK Explorer was an early stage business (not a start up) that had one contract to provide the Youth Hostel Association with internet-access terminals in approximately 30 hostels around the UK. As is so often the case with start-ups and particularly in the IT related sector, this business was being operated out of an extremely small kitchen on the second floor flat in West London.

The business provided internet-terminals, being a desk, chair and computer owned by the company, offering email access in high footfall areas where people tended to be passing, waiting or sitting around. The business was producing limited revenue, was loss making and although cash generating, required significant additional capital to expand their purchase of equipment and speed up the number of installations, as well as providing business premises.

During my initial review, due diligence, and as the days progressed during negotiation of the Shareholder Agreement, I became more comfortable with my decision as the Founders took a balanced and pragmatic approach to the negotiation of the Shareholder Agreement.

In hindsight, the following gave me overall comfort during my review and my decision to invest:

◆ *Managing Director was highly numerate and a good strategic thinker, having been a previous city analyst in both the UK and Australia;*

◆ *IT Director had good, practical, hands on, IT skills proven in a number of big international businesses;*

◆ *The two Founders were clean cut, sensible, level headed, had a sense of humour and were fun to communicate with;*

◆ *The business had its first contract in operation and was producing revenue;*

◆ *I could help with introductions into hospitality locations, a sector in which I had been operating for over 23 years;*

◆ *I had contacts in the financial world, my accounting and strategic experience, company acquisition and sale, and fund raising experience;*

◆ *The business concept was partly proven and appeared to be sound, although there was some market competition;*

◆ *Business model was simple and potentially lucrative;*

◆ *Upside to the business could have been the ability to sell advertising space on the terminals once there was sufficient coverage in the UK, although the Founders never believed they were likely to obtain this additional revenue and this was not included in their business plan;*

◆ *Founders had invested their own funds to get the business to this stage and given up good jobs showing their commitment;*

◆ *Funds to be provided were for capital expenditure and very little working capital;*

◆ *Founders salary expectations were reasonable at £30,000 per annum;*

◆ *Exit opportunity was most likely to be a trade sale to an information technology company; and lastly but not least*

◆ *A good "gut feeling" about the opportunity.*

There is a lot to be said for a good "gut feeling"!

I agreed that I would invest the full amount of the required funds for 30% of the enlarged equity and they produced the Shareholder Agreement that we adapted through negotiation. I believed that the 30% was an equitable stake and as I had a capital gains tax liability from another business sale, I decided to limit my equity level to 30% so that I could take advantage of the UK Enterprise Investment Scheme. This suited the two Founders as this enabled them to hold onto 70% of the equity.

They found a shop premises in West London, which they fitted out on a very small budget, as an internet-shop through which they planned to cover the costs of the premises. This provided a basement for their workshop, bench testing of the computers prior to installation, and some office space at the back of the shop. This gave them a professional place to operate out of in central London, to which they could bring clients, although it was anticipated that the internet-shop part would never cover all the costs, which later proved to be correct as more competition opened up in the immediate area.

The business model was that the company provided the hardware and software for the equipment to accept coins, and later through ongoing development credit card access, and effectively rented space in high footfall areas. Some software installations were "white labeled" if requested.

The company received approximately 10% to 20% of the gross takings above an agreed minimum level of revenue, based on a three years contract. The company had the right to remove the equipment if a certain level of revenue was not achieved, and it was up to the landlord to actively make sure they sold the service, with some leaflet support from UK Explorer. In the case of the locations in the airports, the percentage share of the gross takings was lower, but the volume of the takings was more than double.

In the airports, it was interesting that initially the location of our installations were tucked away from the shopping areas, and signage by the airports was restricted, but eventually these issues were overcome as the airport management began to understand the amount of revenue this space generated.

The business model turned out to be excellent as the initial payback was just over one year, and this gradually fell over the five years of operation as the cost of the hardware and telecommunications were continually falling, resulting in even better returns. We replaced and updated hardware within three years, or earlier where we had high usage, added LED screens as hardware improved and recruited a programmer as we continued to development the software.

On my advice, the Founders implemented a three months weekly forward cash forecast that was updated on a weekly basis to avoid any cash shortfall surprises, and I have subsequently implemented this in other businesses, including other Angel investments. In addition, the performance of each terminal's weekly revenue was monitored, so that appropriate action could be taken where required.

I found them a freelance accountant, so they could run a payroll and monthly management accounts were regularly prepared on a timely basis for our monthly board meetings. I did not really rely on this in the early days as we generally met once a week, to review revenue performance and the level of forward projected cash, either formally or over a beer.

We started to gear up the operation, recruiting essential staff, constantly improving the software and adding many new sites, which included other youth hostels, hotels, cruise liners and airports that were generating substantial cash. However, with the speed of installations it became evident that further funding was required as this was consuming considerable cash resources, despite the good cash generation from the established installations.

Once the staff had proved themselves after a period of time, they were granted shares in the company as a further incentive, and they were very pleased when we did sell the company as they achieved a cash windfall as well as most of the staff transferring across to the purchaser.

We explored the ability to obtain a bank loan for hardware purchases without success (same problems as now in 2010/11!), and even under the UK government's Small Firms Loan Guarantee Scheme. Instead we finance leased some of the hardware until we reached a level that the leasing companies refused to continue to provide this type of finance. This was expensive funding but gave us the ability to continue expanding without diluting our shareholdings.

We held two further small friends and family fund raises during the first four years, to which I contributed to on both occasions, to minimize the dilution my equity stake.

We also looked at the possibility of acquiring other similar businesses, preferably for our shares rather than for cash, but after looking at any number of opportunities, their operations were often less professional than ours and too small to make a major impact. We also could not see the value of acquiring old hardware, often two or more years old, their software that would be replaced with our own, and contracts that we could competitively replace. As a result, acquisitions turned out not to be an attractive proposition for us and a number of the businesses we looked at later failed through lack of investment.

We believed that our product/service that enabled the user to sit down to send emails, browse, play games and in some locations print (particularly in the airports) was a better solution than the internet terminals that you had to stand up at to use, such as the vandal proof steel units British Telecom installed in London phone boxes, and those that were in railway stations and other similar installations in the airports.

One unexpected success we had, contrary to the initial expectations of the Founders, was that we did manage to obtain advertising revenue at this stage, although it was small in relationship to the whole revenue. However, I am fairly certain that this would have grown to a reasonable amount after winning the British Airport Authority ("BAA") contract referred to below.

We were approached by a number of parties overseas to provide our internet-terminal solution, seen on visits to UK airports, but we did not believe we could logistically handle this without forming some sort of joint venture or licensing. We did set up a joint venture with a German company who purchased the hardware and licensed the software but this lasted no more than a year with no loss to ourselves. This does put into perspective the need to ensure adequate resources are focused on operating overseas before setting up operations in other countries.

After an initial year of lobbying, we had achieved installations in most of the UK airports, including the BAA airports. Following on from this success, the Founders lobbied the BAA personnel for more than two years for the opportunity to replace the other internet-terminal operators, who had internet-terminal installations at which one had to stand to use the equipment. However, as in all large businesses, there was a constant change of the personnel that we had to communicate with, until eventually BAA decided to put the internet-terminal business out to tender.

After an appraisal of the BAA tender requirements and the large number of installations required around the country, which were significantly more numerous than our existing installations, and with the likelihood of there being more locations available over time, we estimated that the capital cost could be as much as £500,000.

This was a major challenge and on that basis, despite the cash flow being generated by existing installations, there was a need to raise additional funds. We found what was then a small London venture capital fund, now called YFM Equity Partners, which had interests in the sector that we operated in and who provided capital to early stage businesses. We negotiated a capital injection of £250,000 for a 10% equity stake with the ability to draw a further £250,000 in a repayable, interest-bearing loan, if required.

This led to a requirement that Michael Kennedy, one of the Investment Directors, received our monthly management accounts, annual reports and attended our board meetings and AGMs. In addition, we were in constant dialogue and they received our weekly revenue reports and required that they signed off on major capital expenditure, etc.

In most early stage businesses this would have been a problem, but fortunately the Founders had all previous annual accounts audited each year, set up a robust weekly revenue report against target, usage statistics and a monthly management reporting system influenced by myself. However, the Founders fully understood the need for this and a professional approach required in these areas.

All this preparation, effort and hard work paid off, and we won the tender for all the BAA airports, while retaining the regional airports that BAA did not control. The Founders managed to complete all these installation within six months for under £350,000 and we did not have to draw on the venture capital company loan, due to the strong cash flow generated by our existing installations. However, that safety net had given us the confidence to responsibly make such a large tender without risk of under capitalization.

As the business was performing well and installations were proceeding to plan, we were fortunate that relationship with the venture capital fund representative, Mike Kennedy, was good and they were encouraging with little interference. However, if we had under performed, the situation would have definitely resulted in more regular contact and interference!

One day the Founders approached me, approximately six months after completing the BAA installations, to advise that they wanted to sell the business. Although I would have liked to see a full year benefit from BAA installations, after some discussion, it became clear that strategically the timing was likely to be correct. This was further emphasized when the Cloud purchased the communication rights in all the BAA airports for a very large sum of money before we decided to sell the business. We risked revenue dilution from the use of wi-fi, particularly in the airports and hotels, from Blackberry mobiles and now iPhones, iPads and a host of similar mobile phones and tablets. It turned out that the timing for a trade sale was the correct decision and "I take my hat off" to the Founders for their insight!

Richard Stubbs discussed this with Michael Kennedy of YFM Equity Partners and they received a 30% internal rate of return ("IRR"), having only held their investment for little more than a six months. This was the second time I had been involved with and an investor in a company where a venture capital firm had achieved their 30% IRR!

We held beauty parades for a number of financial advisors in our sector and appointed Andrew Harrington of AHV Associates LLP as our financial advisor to assist with the sale. They kept the potential interested companies at arms length, and did an excellent job. We had a number of potential purchasers and the purchaser with the highest cash offer, our having declined to take equity in the purchaser, completed their due diligence within three weeks over the Christmas/New Year period, and the sale was completed in mid January 2005.

The fast due diligence period was aided by the fact that the annual accounts had been audited every year since formation and the administration of all the contracts and company documentation were in good shape.

UK Explorer was sold to Spectrum Interactive plc that operates the phone boxes in the UK and Germany and through acquiring our company, enabled them to list their company on AIM. The internet-terminal business now forms an increasingly important part of their business while they experience a declining telephone box business.

This business was successfully traded between 1999 and 2005, through the dotcom boom and bust, because it had a sensible management team, had a simple business model and stuck to its business model.

All our shareholders and staff were delighted with the outcome after five years of developing the business in which we all had fun. This I believe gives you an idea of what Angel investing should be about.

Unfortunately, after one of the Founders buying a boat and both taking a six-month break together sailing from the UK to New Zealand, the two Founders decided to stay in New Zealand and Australia respectively, and it is unlikely we will be able to invest together in the future primarily due to my decision to only invest in companies based in my locality!

Actual case study – unsuccessful exit

I was approached by the husband of a Serbian lady, both of whom I had met on numerous occasions before, as I was reviewing whether to invest in his trading business selling liquor, fruit juices, and bottled water imported from Serbia. As mentioned in chapter 3, this is a business that I will not now invest in due to the fierce competition and wafer thin margins after marketing and distribution costs.

However, there are plenty of examples of start-ups in this sector that do succeed, such as Innocent smoothies and Blackwood Gin and Vodka, where the latter raised significant capital and opened a new distillery on one of Scotland's islands. Interestingly, my decision not to invest proved correct as her husbands' business was wound down due to problems with the suppliers who promised financial support but did not deliver.

Her proposition was for me to provide £50,000 of seed money to start up a business of "matchmaking for millionaires" based in London. I am unable to disclose names of the Entrepreneur or the business name, as the business is still operational. As this was a small investment, there were other high-end matchmaking businesses in the market, and as this would be very interesting, I thought this was worth a punt for 25% of the equity!

This investment sounds relatively little, but this was all that was needed to significantly enhance an existing website while she worked from her home. Her husband had worked in the IT sector before starting his drinks trading business and had developed the website up to this stage. The reason for this small amount of funds was that millionaires would be paying from between £30,000 and £60,000 in advance for twelve months contracted support, depending upon the level of service. The £30,000 was for the match making service whereas the £60,000 would be for the match making service and PA support for the millionaire to organize travel and in some cases travel as a companion with them.

This lady was a professional psychiatrist and the business consisted of attracting millionaires, meeting the millionaire in their home or possibly their office, assessing their well being and to establish what sort of partner and interests they were looking for, collecting the up front fee and a signature on a contract for twelve months. In addition, the visit was also to establish that their actual lifestyle supported the fact that they were millionaires, as well as establishing whether there were any emotional issues following perhaps a previous divorce, etc.

This business required absolute
discretion and confidentiality

Generally, these millionaires were very successful Entrepreneurs that had put all their energy and life into their businesses, often resulting in their partners divorcing them where they had been married, and where their friends were closely connected with their business, and they had finally and successfully sold their business. After this, they discovered their business friends fell away and they were of a certain age where meeting the right kind of potential partners in bars and clubs was not to their liking.

The business also had a website to collect details of potential partners, who were generally ordinary well educated people, who had the opportunity to be introduced to these millionaires if they were selected as possible partners by this business. These people paid a small joining fee, and this was essentially a lottery to meet a millionaire! These people were selected from their details from the website database, they were also met and interviewed by a psychiatrist for suitability and if chosen, a meeting would be arranged over dinner in a top restaurant.

It was very interesting to observe that more female millionaires than male millionaires signed up for this service, in a ratio of approximately two female to one male. However, the business quite quickly achieved the first successful match with a male millionaire who was the first to sign up for the service! This was very fortunate as we were able to persuade this couple to publically endorse our service.

This female/male ratio was also experienced for those people who registered on the website. This led to a shortage of suitable male partners available to match to the female millionaires, and the advertising program had to be targeted to increase the number of males registering on to the website.

The millionaire would meet potential partners through an introduction by their contact in the business, which I will loosely call their "Handler", at a top end restaurant, and the other person would be properly introduced to break the ice, taking away any uncertainty for both parties, and if requested by the female the handler would stay on longer.

In addition, we held events at which all the millionaires and selected partners could socialize and meet up together. These events were theatre evenings, sporting events, dinner, etc. of a high standard to match the expectations of the millionaire members. The service provided to the millionaires included access 24 hours a day with their handler, and if they wished, dress advice, grooming advice, physiological advice, and any other service which they required and paid for.

This is a very people intensive business

With these limited funds, the business was being operated on a "bootstrapped" basis, and the initial advertising to attract millionaires had to be cautiously managed so as not to run out of money. We trialed advertising in Private Eye and the Financial Times weekend magazine "How to Spend it" which were successful and led to a number of millionaires paying their annual fee in advance. This led to more advertising activity in other publications on a trial basis, but still within the constraints of having to conserve funds to provide a service over twelve months.

She managed to generate and obtain tremendous free PR herself in many magazines, newspaper publications and TV programs, as this was a topic of public interest that many people appeared very interested in, which generated plenty of enquiries.

We had meetings with a number of small potential PR firms and our experience was that they all "over promised and under delivered", despite being paid a monthly retainer. These PR firms were recruited because we wished to increase exposure in addition to that being generated by the Entrepreneur. There is no doubt, in my mind, that there is nothing better than the energy of the Entrepreneur conveying the message and generating their own PR.

On my advice, she implemented a 12 month forward weekly forecast with help from her husband, which enabled her to manage how much money could be spent on advertising, website costs, PR and overheads. I suspect that this would not have happened without my intervention and will have saved her business from failure in these early months. I also introduced her to an outsourced accountant, outside London, to process the staff payroll and produce monthly management accounts, having had a good previous experience of using this accountant's services.

As the Entrepreneur was very astute, but had not really had any real experience of running a business herself, we agreed that we would have a meeting every week on a Saturday morning, to avoid diluting her time during the working week. At these meetings we reviewed the forward cash forecasts, her excellent PR progress, leads from the advertising and the recruitment success, as well as coming up with fresh ideas to develop the business. I also attended the interview of staff to be employed, potential support services for our millionaires, such a program under consideration with Quintessentially and such similar services.

One day, she approached me to put in additional investment, as she wanted to buy a Mercedes car and establish consulting rooms in Mayfair. I was partly sympathetic to the fact that she had to use serviced offices for meetings, interviewing staff and likely candidates for matching with the millionaires. However, I expressed my concern, as I did not see the need for a car when one could be rented, while running a business on a bootstrapped basis. I felt that it was too early to incur this type of expenditure and I left the meeting saying I would reluctantly consider her request.

In order to minimize my exposure to an additional capital injection, I talked to an American friend of mine living in London, who had successfully sold a media business, and would have brought an additional skill to this business. We had kept in touch as he had indicated that he wanted to join me as an investor when I found a suitable opportunity.

I introduced him to the Entrepreneur and after numerous meeting during which my friend did his due diligence, we decided that we would equally invest a total of £100,000 for a further 25% of her equity that would give us 50% of the equity in her business. However, my friends' preference was that we own a total of 51% of the equity (i.e. control) that I managed to persuade him not to pursue.

My friend asked some very probing questions about her personal situation to establish her commitment that upset her, and when we made our proposal she was not willing to consider this. In the end, her husband leased a Mercedes saloon at his own cost! This was when it became evident to me that she was in this business to raise her profile, rub shoulders with millionaires and provide a life style for herself. While I had no personal problem with this, it really was not an ideal situation for a Business Angel, which I will revisit below.

During this time, our weekly meetings became bi-monthly meetings, and then less frequently as she was apparently not available. One day her husband called me, after I was continually chasing her for a meeting, and he advised that she felt that the meetings were a waste of time and that she was not receiving any benefit from them, which I suspect was partly as the result of the failure to accept our additional financing proposal.

A few weeks later, we met up and she proposed buying out my equity with a marginal benefit for myself. I accepted this without argument, despite this not being structured in a tax efficient way for myself. She advised me that there was no other investor and if so, I suspect this will have been paid out of her client fees paid in advance.

Well before this, I had discussed with her the possibility, in the future, of the potential development of her business as a franchise model based in major cities of the world with little additional capital required. We had previously had enquiries from millionaires in Dubai and Nairobi that indicated there was the potential for an international business, and as I had good international business experience, I could have contributed a lot to the development of a larger business.

I had some limited knowledge of franchising, as I had previously spent some time reviewing what was required to set up a franchise operation. This would have entailed making sure that the franchisee's had a similar professional background to herself, as well as very good personal skills, which may have proved to be difficult to achieve. This was ultimately, why I was interested in her business model as well as the fact that this business should have been materially cash flow positive.

I am afraid that this was not to be the case, as I strongly suspect that besides providing financial security, and that she wanted to be seen in high society rubbing shoulders with millionaires, have the resources to run a prestige car and have a Mayfair apartment. The business is still operational, now operating out of a Knightsbridge location and I wish her well.

What are the lessons I have learned from this experience?

- *Avoid opportunities that could turn out to be life style businesses;*
- *Never take 51% of a business for the sake of control;*
- *Avoid astute people who have no real business experience;*
- *Ensure that the Entrepreneur's vision is aligned with that of the Business Angel;*
- *Never invest just because it is an immaterial amount; and*
- *Always be the sole investor.*

CHAPTER ELEVEN

Conclusion

Many Business Angels are retirees and/or experienced business people who have generated wealth from previous business success, wish to create further wealth, and give something back to society by assisting Entrepreneurs to successfully develop a business, which can also be great fun.

While it is fun to be involved with highly energized and enthusiastic Entrepreneurs supporting the development of a new business or idea, it can be very time consuming for the Business Angel who wishes to be more actively supportive of the business they have invested in. The reward is often not just for money for the time, but the reward of seeing the sense of achievement by the Entrepreneur as well as achieving an agreed end game.

This is extremely high risk investing and in my view you should not pursue Angel investing unless you are willing to loose the investment funds you have allocated to Angel investing, have prior business experience and are willing to mentor/advise the Entrepreneur.

The dotcom boom bust gave the public a perception that university graduates could set up an internet-based business with a laptop, make a fortune without any tangible assets to raise significant capital based on a five years plan, without property, franchises, revenues, patents and profits.

As we all know, life is not like that, and although perceptions changed after the dotcom bust, it seems some have forgotten the pain since then. There appears to be an indication of over excitement once again around this sector and the possibility of over pricing opportunities once again. There are very few real business successes such as Facebook, Google and Amazon, amongst the thousands of early stage companies that are set up and fail. This underlines the high-risk of Angel investing, with most businesses never reaching a sustainable business size.

In my view, Syndicate investing throwing say between £10,000 to £50,000 over a whole range of different start up and early stage businesses, often 10 or more, will not produce the returns you could achieve by focusing on one or two businesses to which you can add previous business experience.

Angel investing can be fun
as well as rewarding

Business Funding Cycle

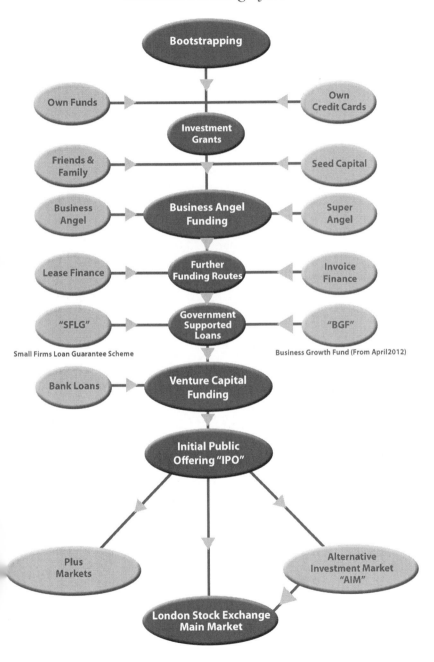

Bootstrapping

Own Funds

Own Credit Cards

Investment Grants

Friends & Family

Seed Capital

Business Angel

Business Angel Funding

Super Angel

Lease Finance

Further Funding Routes

Invoice Finance

"SFLG"

Government Supported Loans

"BGF"

Small Firms Loan Guarantee Scheme

Business Growth Fund (From April 2012)

Bank Loans

Venture Capital Funding

Initial Public Offering "IPO"

Plus Markets

Alternative Investment Market "AIM"

London Stock Exchange Main Market

Business Angel Investment Process

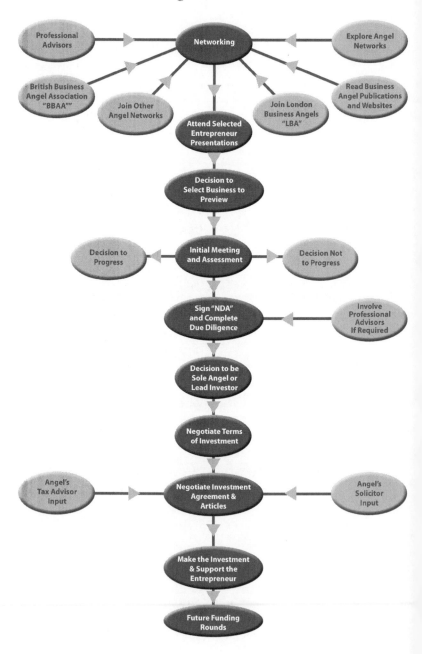

List of UK Angel Networks

BBAA Member Networks

- *Advantage Business Angels*
- *Beer and Partners*
- *Beer and Young*
- *Central England Business Angels*
- *Connect London*
- *Creative Arts Investment Network*
- *Entrust*
- *Envestors*
- *Finance South East*
- *Growth Investment East Midlands*

- *Halo Northern Ireland*
- *Kingston Business Angels*
- *London Business Angels*
- *Minerva Business Angel Network*
- *Octopus Ventures*
- *Oxford Early Investments*
- *Oxfordshire Investment Opportunity Network*
- *Thames Valley Investment Network*
- *Xenos*
- *Yorkshire Association of Business Angels*

Other Angel Networks

◆ *LINC Scotland*

◆ *Cambridge Angels*

◆ *Cambridge Capital*

◆ *ISIS Angel Network*

◆ *Angels 5K*

◆ *BIG*

◆ *Hotbed*

◆ *Hotspurs*

◆ *Seraphim*

◆ *MMC Ventures*

◆ *Pi Capital*

◆ *Angel Investment Network*

About the Author

Jonathan Harrison is a Chartered Accountant (FCA) and a Fellow of the Institute of Directors (FInstD) with experience in quoted and unquoted companies. Previously he spent 16 years at Intercontinental Hotels Corporation, USA, (now UK based IHG plc.) where he held various executive financial roles covering Europe, Middle East and Africa. He also managed the financial integration of Grand Metropolitan Hotels Limited into Intercontinental Hotels.

In 1989 he joined the Boddington Group plc, as Finance Director establishing a new division of branded hotels and restaurants. He later became Operations Director of Village Leisure Hotels responsible for the operation of six leisure hotels. While still at the Boddington Group, having proved himself as a trouble-shooter, he was assigned as Finance Director of Country House Retirement Homes Limited and within 18 months nearly doubled the number of nursing homes to 31, later leading the sale of the business by auction to BUPA.

In March 1997 he led a £92m management buy-in of 25 hotels from Queens Moat House plc with Duke Street Capital, and six months later managed the refinancing of County Hotels Group plc with a dual listed bond offering in Luxembourg. In January 1999 the company was successfully sold to Regal Hotel Group plc. achieving a 30% internal rate of return.

In 1999 he joined Topnotch Health Clubs plc, overseeing a fast track eleven week listing on AIM in March 2000, obtained additional bank finance and grew the company from five to twenty health clubs within 18 months.

In 1999 he became seed capital investor and Non Executive Director ("NED") of UK Explorer Limited. After obtaining venture capital investment, winning a major contract, he successfully completed a trade sale in January 2005. As a Business Angel, he also invested in one start-up and three other early stage businesses and continues to look for similar opportunities.

In 2004 he joined a new mineral exploration company as Finance Director and oversaw the listing of Sirius Minerals plc (formerly Sirius Exploration plc) on AIM in August 2005 with a £2m market capital. After a series of acquisitions, the company became the only UK listed potash exploration company, and in January 2011 he retired from the board with a market capital of £150m. During this time, as Finance Director, he also oversaw the listing of World Mining Services Limited (not related with Sirius Minerals) on Plus and the company set up of a coal briquetting plant in Poland and held an investment in a mining technology business.

He is currently, NED of Canadian mineral exploration company, Fundy Minerals Limited, a start-up USA social penny arcade company, Affinity Arcade Corporation.

In 2008 he published a book in his own name, "Life's Hop, Skip and a Jump" (available from **www.lulu.com** and **www. amazon.com**) describing his unique experiences travelling around the world with Intercontinental Hotels, his experiences migrating from the corporate ladder to being an entrepreneurial Finance Director with experience of listing, acquiring and selling companies, and investing in early stage companies. He also has a photographic website **www.jonathanharrisonimages.com** containing photographs taken travelling around the World.

Testimonials

"A good Business Angel is like a demanding parent, an investor is more like a lazy banker"

Winton G. Rossitor, Chairman and Managing Director of JazzyMedia and Weight Wins.

Jonathan Harrison is one of the shrewdest Angel Investors that I Know. I have worked with him on a number of deals both large and small and we have made and lost money together: fortunately much more than the latter. If you want to learn about Angel Investing from one of the masters of the art, I can do no better than quote Gordon Gekko from Wall Street II: "BUY THIS BOOK!"

Richard Poulden, Deputy Chairman, Sirius Minerals Plc, Dubai.

"Jonathan Harrison was our seed capital investor in UK Explorer and provided consistent support, advice and encouragement, found us an outsourced accountant and contributed to the management reporting. In view of his past business experience, he also assisted us with the successful trade sale"

Richard Stubbs, Head of Equities – Investments, TOWER, New Zealand.

"Jonathan Harrison is a rarity, a senior finance person with business flair, yet a common-sense person. It's typical of Jonathan Harrison's character that he's endeavoured to help others by sharing his experiences. He's truly an angel on the side of the entrepreneurs."

Professor Michael Mainelli, Executive Chairman, Z/Yen Group Limited.

*I have had the pleasure of being seated on several Boards with **Jonathan Harrison** over the years. He is always most attentive, looking at the big picture while focusing in on the importance of the minutiae. He is the consummate fiduciary, with an even keel."*

Jeffrey W. Michel, Southwood Partners Inc. (USA)

2657084R00055

Printed in Great Britain
by Amazon.co.uk, Ltd.,
Marston Gate.